Series 1
Racism and the U.S. Church

Vital
Conversations
On Race, Culture, and Justice

RELIGION & RACE

General Commission on Religion and Race

THE UNITED METHODIST CHURCH

Table of Contents

Series 1: Racism and the U.S. Church

Preface

Conversations around race can be uncomfortable for most of us. The church is no exception.

The General Commission on Religion and Race of The United Methodist Church offers *Vital Conversations: Race, Culture, and Justice* as a way to begin a dialogue, face our misconceptions and fears, and move deliberately to spiritual, community, and social transformation.

The General Commission on Religion and Race offers resources to facilitate, resource, guide, and support discussions on how to move to efficacy, justice, and courageous positive action. Our vision is to invite and lead the church into new conversations about our relevance and our calling from God to serve a world that is far different than when we began our work.

The commission works to build the capacity of The United Methodist Church to be more relevant to more people, younger people, and more diverse people in order to nurture disciples of Jesus Christ who will transform the world for the better. Our ministry model provides resources for congregations and church leaders to increase intercultural competency, institutional equity, and vital conversations.

We recommend that Series 1: Racism and the U.S. Church be conducted in eight sessions:

- Session 1: Introduction
- Sessions 2–8: Videos and Discussion

The introduction and closing sessions may be shorter or longer in length, depending on the group. The seven core sessions are designed to last about ninety minutes, including the videos. Each video runs twenty minutes or less. Eight to ten people in the group are recommended for greater intimacy and participation.

The flow of the core meetings is:

- **Check-in**—how your week was and prayer requests
- **Prayer**—based in part on check-in
- **Video viewing**—of the seven presenters
- **Discussion**—based on questions
- **Next week**—expectations and what is to come
- **Closing prayer**—in unison

We are delighted that you have joined us to discuss the issues related to faith, culture, and justice in the church and world today through small groups.

The videos by the speakers are available at www.gcorr.org/series/vc1.

Getting Started

Anyone who claims to live in God's light and hates a brother or sister is still in the dark. It's the person who loves brother and sister who dwells in God's light and doesn't block the light from others. But whoever hates is still in the dark, stumbles around in the dark, doesn't know which end is up, blinded by the darkness.

~ 1 John 2:9–11 (MSG)

The assertion that "We are in this together" sometimes sounds empty and inauthentic, overused and void of true feeling and real action, especially at a time when our society seems so divided along lines of ideology, race, class, nation, culture, and ethnicity.

Yet God calls us, as Christians, to come together and "get along," be in relationship as sisters and brothers in the light, rejecting the darkness, rejecting the sin of racism.

Moving into the light, we ask church leaders and participants to come together in humility, vulnerability, and willingness to have open conversations about race and racism. The first steps of organizing a group and coming together may be one of the most courageous things many of us have ever attempted. Committing to eight weeks of conversation brings us closer to transforming the world for Christ by dismantling racism.

This guide is for the facilitators of the group who should prepare in spiritual and practical ways:

Prayer
Racism and segregation go back centuries in the United States in the form of enslavement of Africans, colonizing and exterminating Native Americans, forcing Japanese Americans into internment camps, and more. We face centuries of systemic and institutionalized racism, but do not be daunted by this history of racism. God can transform all. Small groups, modeled on Jesus' call to and teaching of the twelve disciples, are an important means for change.

Before your study group even gathers members and sets the first meeting date, be in agreement with at least one person to join you in praying for our nation concerning racism, for the upcoming group, and for each potential member.

Look to Psalm 7 as a foundational prayer for justice and a spiritual starting point, continuing to look to parts of the prayer throughout the sessions for the small group.

While praying as you start this study group, ask God to reveal other needs specific to members of the group. Pray that God will help:

- soften the hearts of the people in your setting who will be resistant to a small group that focuses on racial justice,
- ready people who would never join such a group but do so ultimately,
- prepare the hearts and spirits of facilitators and future members,
- grant wisdom to everyone directly and indirectly connected to the group,
- identify group members,
- knit the group together as the eight weeks go by,
- make the Holy Spirit central in directing and leading the group.

Audience

Racism is pervasive and destructive so the audience for this small group is anyone and everyone. That said, many specific groups and individuals would benefit: local church leadership, Sunday schools, young adults, Wesley Foundations/campus ministries, annual conference cabinets and staff, racially diverse mission and ministry groups, seminary classes, groups of lay leaders and local pastors in districts and conferences, affinity groups for people of all races/ethnicities, United Methodist Women, United Methodist Men, missions, and more.

Choosing or Deciding on Facilitators

Anyone can facilitate a group who is courageous enough to face and deal with the tensions, emotional struggle, and even possible recrimination that will come out of directly discussing racism as a group.

Suggested Reading for the Facilitator(s)

Some advance reading is recommended before launching a group:

- Ronald Takaki's *A Different Mirror: A History of Multicultural America*
- Peggy McIntosh's *White Privilege: Unpacking the Invisible Knapsack* (available at http://nationalseedproject.org/white-privilege-unpacking-the-invisible-knapsack)
- Shelly Tochluk's *Witnessing Whiteness: The Need to Talk about Race and How to Do It*
- Ta-Nehisi Coates's *Between the World and Me*

Inviting People to Participate in the Study

- **Pray**—ask God for direction on who and how to invite.
- **Be inclusive**—invite the people you know, who look like you, but also go beyond one's comfort zone asking new people who look and think differently.
- **Ask**—be bold taking a step of faith, asking an acquaintance or stranger to join.
- **Communicate**—a personal invitation in person, by phone, or via e-mail is preferred. You may also promote participation with posters, e-blasts, Facebook, Twitter, and in-person announcements at gatherings.
- **Be patient**—answers may not be immediate or come at all because people need room to pray and reflect on what will be a challenging journey, facing and acting against racism.
- **Trust in God**—by faith, a group will form, while continuing to prepare the details and content for the sessions.
- **Be flexible**—be willing to make changes midstream in planning, hearing from God, and listening to people around you and potential members.

Videos and Questions

As the group watches each video together, invite discussion based on questions provided for each session. Share thoughts, impressions, and ideas. Keep in mind it is easy to drift away from the difficult and uncomfortable topic of race and racism by deflecting and turning to other themes and issues.

When relevant, recognize possible parallels with other forms of bias, institution "isms," and forms of oppression, but keep the group focused on the grappling with racism.

Session 1: Introduction

Check-in:
Ask about everyone's week, along with prayer requests for joys and sorrows.

Prayer
During the first week, the facilitator should pray rather than request a volunteer. The first day of a small group can be challenging and awkward. People may feel put on the spot being asked to pray. Focusing on racism further deepens the discomfort of the first days of small group. Consider the following parts of a traditional prayer that might make a difficult theme of racism and justice easier to embrace, keeping in mind that prayer requires no formula.

- **Adoration**—Praise God for being the Almighty One, for gathering the group to deal directly with the difficult subject of racism.
- **Confession**—Admit that we have all sinned, and that racism is also a sin.
- **Thanksgiving**—Express gratitude to God for the opportunity to have frank, safe discussions about racism as Christians.
- **Supplication**—Acknowledge joys and pray for sorrows group members shared at the start of the session.

Covenant
Small groups should create a covenant for the emotional and spiritual safety of each member and the group, along with concrete means of setting boundaries. Because of the sensitive nature of having conversations about racism, a group covenant becomes more important.

Consider the Following:
We join together to have new conversations about our relevance and our calling from God to serve a world that we pray will be far different as we begin our work fighting racism. We will build the capacity of our group to be more relevant to more people, younger people, and more diverse people in order to nurture disciples of Jesus Christ who will transform the world for the better. Our hope is that when our group comes to a close, some or all of us will begin new small groups, expanding the ministry of anti-racism. We will strive to get to know one another, pray together, learn together, serve and do outreach and justice together, keeping in mind that God is the leader and center of our small group.

Using the Vital Conversations: Race, Culture, and Justice videos and conversation, we will do all these things, developing a better understanding of racism and the tools to dismantle racism. I agree to participate, faithfully attending the sessions, reading, contributing, and caring for the needs of the others in the group. I will hold in confidence any personal information that is shared in this group.

Signature _____

Name _____

Date _____

The group is encouraged to draw from this covenant or come up with something new. Specific themes based on group discussion can be used to encourage conversation in drafting a covenant: respect multiple viewpoints; own your intentions and impact; challenge in love; take risks; practice active listening and speak from one's own experience; assert opinions without attacking other group members; affirm frustration, confusion, and fear; and maintain confidentiality.

Face Test: Do I Have the Full Picture?
Spend 15 minutes doing the "Face Test."

The body of Christ is multicolored, made up of thousands of languages and experiences, multiracial and interclass. But our upbringing, family, friends, schools, and churches—from which we develop our worldview—are often not so diverse. Did your background expose you to the many textures of God's human family? Draw one component of a human face for every "yes" answer you get for the following statements (eye, eye, nose, mouth, ear, ear, and hair). If you can't draw a whole face, draw as far as you can, and be prepared to discuss the ones you could draw.

1. At least one member of my immediate family (parents, siblings, brother/sister-in-law, grandparents) is from a racial/ethnic group other than my own (meaning at least one of their parents is Asian/Pacific Islander, Latino/a, Native American/indigenous to the Americas, African-American, or of African descent or Anglo/White/European descent).
2. At least one family on my block (one out of about ten homes) is of a racial/ethnic group other than my own.
3. At least one of my close friends (you know their parents and/or their phone number is programmed into your cell phone, etc.) is from a racial/ethnic group other than my own.
4. The church I attend is racially mixed (at least 10 percent of the members are of a racial group other than my own).
5. The schools I attend(ed) are/were racially mixed (at least 10 percent of the student body are from a racial group or groups other than my own).
6. Of my ten closest friends (i.e., the last people you want to see before you pass on), at least one is from a racial/ethnic group other than my own.
7. I grew up in a home where I never heard my parents or siblings say a negative word about groups of people by race or ethnicity (i.e., "Those dumb Puerto Ricans"; "Jews only care about money"; "She's poor White trash"; "Race-mixing is against the Bible, so you can't date a Black girl," etc.).
8. Of the friends my parent(s) socialize(d) with and regularly invite(d) to our home, at least one is/was from a racial/ethnic/language group other than their own.

Based on the Face Test, discuss how participants were able to create a full face or not. What does this test say about our worldviews and experience when it comes to cross-racial relationships?

Closing Prayer in Unison
Light a candle as a reminder of the Holy Spirit's presence.

Dear God, conversations about racism are difficult. Yet we come together, willing to do the hard work. We thank You, Lord, for this opportunity to enter this safe space to openly share about our national struggle, our global struggle, our church's struggle, and our personal challenges with racism. As we leave one another today, continue to draw our group together, continue to challenge us about racism, and continue to lead us to act. Amen.

Dr. Robin DiAngelo

Deconstructing White Privilege

Dr. Robin DiAngelo is a social scientist and anti-racism educator and the author of *What Does It Mean to Be White? Developing White Racial Literacy*. Director of equity for Sound Generations in the Seattle, Washington, area, Dr. DiAngelo's previous book (with Özlem Sensoy), *Is Everyone Really Equal: An Introduction to Key Concepts in Social Justice Education*, received the Critics' Choice Award by the American Educational Studies Association. Her work on white fragility has appeared in Alternet, Salon.com, NPR, Colorlines, Huffington Post, and the Good Men Project.

Session 2: Deconstructing White Privilege

The poor man and the oppressor have this in common: The Lord gives light to the eyes of both.
~ Proverbs 29:13 (AMP)

Check-in
Ask about everyone's week, along with prayer requests for joys and sorrows.

Open with Prayer

Introduction to *Deconstructing White Privilege* Video
All of us must seek the light of God and the light of truth in recognizing oppression. We begin to do so in this session, which focuses on the oppressive behavior that is born out of white privilege.

Dr. Robin DiAngelo is transparent about white privilege couched in explicit and implicit biases in the video *Deconstructing White Privilege*, the first in a series of *Vital Conversations on Race, Culture, and Justice*.

Dr. DiAngelo describes the most obvious and explicit aspects of racism and white privilege, while going beyond the surface of racism. Her video serves as a foundation on understanding racism and white privilege for the remaining six videos in the *Vital Conversations* series.

Video
Watch *Deconstructing White Privilege*,
http://gcorr.org/vital-conversations-racism-dr-robin-diangelo (21:54).

Discussion Questions

1. What ideas presented by Dr. DiAngelo stood out for you? How does she describe her experience as one who recognizes herself as a white person, especially when it comes to interacting with people of color?
2. How does denying the existence of racism and white privilege perpetuate racial inequality and unequal outcomes? What are explicit and implicit biases? Give some examples from the video along with some of your own.
3. How can identifying the pillars—individualism, universalism, internalized superiority, good/bad binary, segregation, and miseducation—help in challenging racism? What are the next steps?
4. Dr. DiAngelo says we are not "operating in the spiritual realm" when it comes to racial issues. Is this true for Christians, and what does that mean concerning racism and justice both theologically and biblically? Based on our Christian experiences and the Bible, how can we begin to act against inequity and racism?

Closing Prayer in Unison
Light a candle as a reminder of the Holy Spirit's presence.

Most High God, You urge us to advocate for justice for the widowed and the orphaned. For our contemporary times, one form of oppression is against people of color through white privilege. Open our eyes to the impact racism has on the widowed and the orphaned . . . the African-American woman brutalized by the police . . . the Mexican-American student being told derisively to go back to Mexico. Use us to face white privilege and dismantle racism. Amen.

Dr. Miguel de la Torre

Building the Beloved Community

Dr. Miguel de la Torre is a professor of social ethics and Latino/a Studies at the Iliff School of Theology in Denver, Colorado. Born in Cuba and ordained in the Southern Baptist Church, Dr. de la Torre is an engaging speaker, an inspiring scholar and activist, and a prolific author whose books and articles include the popular *Reading the Bible from the Margins* and his newest, *Liberating Sexuality: Justice Between the Sheets*. He has been an expert commentator concerning ethical issues related to Hispanic/Latino religiosity, LBGTQ civil rights, and immigration rights and has appeared in several local, national, and international media outlets. He is well known for his unique approach of religiously analyzing social issues from the perspective of the dispossessed and disenfranchised.

Session 3: Building the Beloved Community

The nonviolent resister must often express his protest through noncooperation or boycotts, but he realizes that noncooperation and boycotts are not ends themselves; they are merely means to awaken a sense of moral shame in the opponent. The end is redemption and reconciliation. The aftermath of nonviolence is the creation of the beloved community, while the aftermath of violence is tragic bitterness.

~ Martin Luther King Jr., 1957

Introduction to *Building the Beloved Community* Video

Dr. Miguel de la Torre's approach to dismantling racism is religiously analyzing social issues from the perspective of the dispossessed and disenfranchised.

In his video ***Building the Beloved Community***, Dr. de la Torre focuses on the church's role in embracing marginalized communities and cultivating a true spirit of multiculturalism. He names racism as a sin.

Video

Watch *Building the Beloved Community*,
http://gcorr.org/church-building-beloved-community (16:44)

Discussion Questions

1. What are some of the barriers within The United Methodist Church to building the beloved community and combatting racism?
2. The United Methodist Church in the United States is 97 percent white. What barriers may prevent or discourage people of color from engaging in our ministries and attending our churches? How does our church (or ministry) rank in terms of bringing in people of color or people of other races and ethnicities?
3. What does Dr. de la Torre say about a "color-blind" approach to issues of racial inclusion and justice? What are the implications of racial color blindness in church?
4. What is the difference between individual versus broader social reconciliation?
5. What does the apostle Paul say about diversifying? What does the Scripture mean for diversifying the church?

Closing Prayer in Unison

Light a candle as a reminder of the Holy Spirit's presence.

Loving God, we have all sinned. We come to You repenting of the sin of racism. God, raise the consciousness of those whites in power who benefit from racism in the world and The United Methodist Church. Transform all of us in this struggle without being defensive. Once minds are opened to sin and forgiveness, may we be reconciled one to another as the beloved community. Amen.

Now there are varieties of gifts, but the same Spirit; and there are varieties of services, but the same Lord; and there are varieties of activities, but it is the same God who activates all of them in everyone.

~ 1 Corinthians 12:4-6 (NRSV)

Reverend Chebon Kernell

Ongoing Acts of Repentance

The Reverend Glen Chebon Kernell Jr. is the executive secretary of Native American and Indigenous Ministries of the General Board of Global Ministries of The United Methodist Church. In this role, he spends half of his time serving as the coordinator for the United Methodist Council of Bishops' effort to fulfill the General Conference resolution mandating an ongoing process to improve relations with indigenous persons through dialogue, study, and local or regional acts of repentance. The other half of his time is spent raising awareness, increasing advocacy, and supporting the empowerment of Native American and indigenous communities globally. Reverend Kernell is an ordained elder in the Oklahoma Indian Missionary Conference.

Session 4: Ongoing Acts of Repentance

Bear fruit worthy of repentance. ~ *Matthew 3:8 (NRSV)*

Check-in
Ask about everyone's week, along with prayer requests for joys and sorrows.

Open with Prayer

Introduction to the *Ongoing Acts of Repentance* Video
Building upon the previous video by Dr. Miguel de la Torre, the Reverend Chebon Kernell calls the church to participate more vigorously in ongoing acts of repentance, justice making and truth telling about the historical and continuing impact of racism, specifically on Native American and indigenous people.

Video

Watch *Ongoing Acts of Repentance*,
http://gcorr.org/ongoing-acts-repentance-featuring-rev-kernell (13:28).

Discussion Questions

1. What is the United Methodist Acts of Repentance movement? How have various groups, particularly indigenous people, reacted to this movement?
2. What forms of racism have indigenous people encountered? What is the meaning of "love thy neighbor as thyself," particularly for indigenous communities and people confronted by racism?
3. What is some of the history of racism against indigenous people? What has this racism meant to indigenous languages? Does history impact us today? What is the impact of spiritual violence?
4. What has your annual conference, district, congregation, or ministry done to follow up on the 2012 Acts of Repentance? If your group is not familiar with the "Acts," what can you do to learn more and inform others in your ministry context?
5. Some non-Native persons ask, "How many times do we have to apologize? When will you be satisfied?" What should be the church's response to these questions?
6. How does working against racism and for justice connect to our Christian discipleship?

Closing Prayer in Unison

Light a candle as a reminder of the Holy Spirit's presence.

Lord Jesus, we humbly come to You repenting of our sins. Let us hear and support our indigenous sisters and brothers who are suffering because of a long history of racism that impacts all of us today. In our relationship with the indigenous community, let repentance move to meaningful action. Amen.

Next Week

Remind group members to read Peggy McIntosh's *White Privilege: Unpacking the Invisible Knapsack* in advance of next week's session: http://nationalseedproject.org/white-privilege-unpacking-the-invisible-knapsack.

Dr. David Anderson Hooker

Meaningful Conversations about Race

Dr. David Anderson Hooker is the professor of the practice of conflict transformation and peacebuilding at the Kroc Institute for International Peace Studies, part of the University of Notre Dame's Keough School of Global Affairs. A consultant with JustPeace, a conflict-transformation ministry within The United Methodist Church, Dr. Hooker is a lawyer, mediator, and facilitator who has worked with communities, governments, and international NGOs on justice making and peace building.

Session 5: Meaningful Conversations about Race

Happy are those who observe justice, who do righteousness at all times.

~ *Psalm 106:3 (NRSV)*

Check-in

Ask about everyone's week, along with prayer requests for joys and sorrows.

Open with Prayer

Introduction to the *Meaningful Conversations about Race* Video

Dr. David Anderson Hooker outlines elements that hinder and help fruitful dialogue on issues of race in the *Meaningful Conversations about Race* video. In doing so, he traces how myths about race define how we function in life, including work and school, in the form of institutional racism. Dr. Hooker says by avoiding the hard conversations about race, we short-circuit any meaningful dialogue that can result in transformation in our lives and across the country.

Video

Watch *Meaningful Conversations about Race*, http://gcorr.org/meaningful-conversations-about-race-featuring-rev-dr-hooker (19:36).

Discussion Questions

1. Dr. Hooker lists three main arguments people make to avoid talking about race and racism. How do these arguments reflect your own lived experience or perspective in life?
2. How do negative feelings affect our willingness and ability to discuss the tough topics of racism, racial injustice, and white privilege?
3. In his dandelion-bluegrass analogy, Dr. Hooker asserts that our systems are not neutral but shaped by biases, tradition, histories, and practices, which is one reason that dandelions are considered weeds to be destroyed, while bluegrass is prized as creating a beautiful lawn. Consider the following list, and discuss how our perceptions of race and racial identity influence what we consider as good/positive/appropriate/traditional appearance of:
   - a dating/marriage partner
   - a hardworking person
   - a safe neighborhood
   - beautiful hair and skin
   - a reliable world leader
   - a cute baby
   - the "all-American" couple
   - the kind of pastor I want in my church
   - a Sunday school teacher
   - artists' renderings of Jesus, Mary, or Moses
   - a stained-glass depiction of Jesus as "The Good Shepherd"
   - a person I would vote for as mayor of my town
4. Dr. Hooker tells his story at the end of the video concerning race and racism. Any similarities or differences in your own story?
5. How do your current local-church experiences in worship, outreach, mission, and witness prepare you to be in community with people of other races? What are some ways you are willing to work in your church to begin building ongoing relationships, Christian community, and space for honest dialogue across racial lines?

Closing Prayer in Unison

Light a candle as a reminder of the Holy Spirit's presence.

Our God on High! Make plain to us what remains invisible to many concerning racist words, actions, and behavior. We seek You, God, to lead us in dismantling institutional racism and inequitable realities based on so many of our false myths. May we join together as Christian sisters and brothers in agreement. Amen.

Come now, let us argue it out.
~ Isaiah 1:18a (NRSV)

Dr. Philip Klinkner

Continued Struggles in American Race Relations

Dr. Philip Klinkner is a political scientist, blogger, and author. He is noted for his work on American politics, especially political parties and elections, race and American politics, and American political history. He is currently the James S. Sherman Professor of Government at Hamilton College in central New York. In his book, *The Unsteady March: The Rise and Decline of Racial Equality in America*, Dr. Klinkner and his coauthor Rogers Smith argue America's record of race relations cannot be categorized as consistent, gradual advancement toward equality but rather as a series of dramatic moments where multiple factors aligned to advance or hinder progress. The book was the winner of the W. E. B. Du Bois Institute's Horace Mann Bond Book Award and was named as a semifinalist for the 2000 Robe F. Kennedy Book Award.

Session 6: Continued Struggles in American Race Relations

And you must be responsible for the bodies of the powerful—the policeman who cracks you with a nightstick will quickly find his excuse in your furtive movements. . . .You cannot forget how much... they transfigured our very bodies into sugar, tobacco, cotton, and gold.

~ Ta-Nehisi Coates, Between the World and Me (2015)

Check-in
Ask about everyone's week, along with prayer requests for joys and sorrows.

Open with Prayer

Introduction to the *Continued Struggles in American Race Relations* Video
In *Continued Struggles in American Race Relations*, Dr. Philip Klinkner confirms that the vestiges of racism for many people of color remain and have not been eradicated. Nor have the practices of institutions in the United States been aligned with democratic ideals of liberty for all. Dr. Klinkner argues that the advance of equality has been unsteady with brief and isolated periods of improvement and long steady stretches of stagnation and retreat.

Video
Watch *Continued Struggles in Race Relations*, http://www.gcorr.org/video/continued-struggles-in-american-race-relations-2/ (11:48)

Discussion Questions
1. What were the three periods of improvement for racial equality in U.S. history? During these periods, what were indicators of progress in equality?
2. From the 1940s, how did advocates for equality make comparisons between the fight for democracy abroad and the lack of democracy for African Americans in the United States?
3. After the wars, how did retrenchment, retreat, and roll-backs increase inequality for African Americans? Why did racist ideology make a comeback after the wars? How was such racist ideology expressed?
4. Based on Dr. Klinkner's research and our own knowledge, what role has the U.S. Christian churches and other religious institutions in the struggles for racial equality? If you were grading the church on forwarding racial justice, what would that grade be? Why?
5. What lessons have the abolitionists taught us in the face of hopelessness in dismantling racism? What can we learn from William Lloyd Garrison, quoted at the end of this session?

Closing Prayer in Unison
Light a candle as a reminder of the Holy Spirit's presence.

Almighty God, thank You for opening our eyes to the relationship between history and our lives today. May we lengthen the stretches of advancements in equality. May we speak up, loudly fighting, and acting quickly, shortening the long periods in which little progress is made against racism. Amen.

On this subject, I do not wish to think, or to speak, or write, with moderation. No! no! Tell a man whose house is on fire to give a moderate alarm; tell him to moderately rescue his wife from the hands of the ravisher; tell the mother to gradually extricate her babe from the fire into which it has fallen; —but urge me not to use moderation in a cause like the present. I am in earnest—I will not equivocate—I will not excuse—I will not retreat a single inch—AND I WILL BE HEARD.
~ William Lloyd Garrison, 1831

Dr. Pamela Lightsey

Intersections of Oppression and Experiences in Ferguson, Missouri

Dr Pamela Lightsey is associate dean for community life and lifelong learning and clinical assistant professor of contextual theology and practice at Boston University School of Theology. She is a well-known scholar, social-justice activist, and military veteran whose research and work has focused on just-war theory, womanist and "queer" theology, and African-American religious history and theology. An ordained elder in The United Methodist Church, she was among the first members of the executive committee for the Soul Repair Project, which studies the role of moral injury on veterans. Her publications include *Our Lives Matter: A Womanist Queer Theology*.

Session 7: Intersections of Oppression and Experiences in Ferguson, Missouri

It is a peculiar sensation, this double-consciousness, this sense of always looking at one's self through the eyes of others, of measuring one's soul by the tape of a world that looks on in amused contempt and pity.

~ W. E. B. Du Bois (1903)

Check-in
Ask about everyone's week, along with prayer requests for joys and sorrows.

Open with Prayer

Introduction to the *Intersections of Oppression and Experiences in Ferguson, Missouri* Video

Dr. Pamela Lightsey explores intersectionality—the overlapping of social categories including race, class, and gender—in the context of her life as a clergywoman, a lesbian, and an African-American woman. In her video *Intersections of Oppression and Experiences in Ferguson, Missouri*, she uses her own history and experience as a lens for analyzing and understanding the racial strife in Ferguson, Missouri.

Video

Watch *Intersections of Oppression and Experiences in Ferguson, Missouri*, http://www .gcorr.org/video/the-intersections-of-oppression-with-rev-dr-pamela-lightsey-2/ (14:40).

Discussion Questions

1. What does Dr. Lightsey's anecdotal experience as a clergywoman, a lesbian, and an African-American woman say about the state of the church when it comes to the intersectionality of gender and ethnicity/race?
2. How can we embrace and act on the doctrine of the Imago Dei relationship to the sacred worth of all people?
3. What does it mean to oppress others when we are all of sacred worth, all part of God's created work?
4. Why are the implications of intersectionality based on social constructs in Ferguson? What have been some of the practical implications for people in Ferguson?
5. How is understanding intersectionality helpful as a tool for social justice activists?
6. How is patriarchy being addressed in leadership roles for African-American women in Ferguson? Why is the shift from patriarchy important, including the history of the U.S. Civil Rights Movement?
7. How has the lesbian, bisexual, gay, transgender, queer (LBGTQ) community qualified the Black Lives Matter movement? What are some places of intersectionality with LBGTQ persons and their allies?
8. What can we do as Christians in response to the oppression of intersectionality?

Closing Prayer in Unison

Light a candle as a reminder of the Holy Spirit's presence.

Christ, our Savior and the Prince of Peace, we pray for all who are in the midst of civil unrest and violence in places like Ferguson. Continue to open our hearts to the implications of intersectionality to people of color oppressed by racism. May we continue to speak up and act on behalf of the oppressed. Amen.

Bishop Cynthia Moore-KoiKoi

Tearing Down Fences in Baltimore

Bishop Cynthia Moore-Koikoi is episcopal leader of the Western Pennsylvania Conference of The United Methodist Church. She was elected in summer 2016, while she was superintendent of the denomination's Baltimore Metropolitan District. She played a key spiritual role in the city in 2015 during the unrest after the death of Freddie Gray in police custody, organizing churches to open their doors and minister to children and families whose schools were closed and to meet other basic needs. She became the face of The United Methodist Church, and church volunteers in red T-shirts were visible walking through neighborhoods, praying for and ministering to people.

Session 8: Tearing Down Fences in Baltimore

Session 8: Tearing Down Fences in Baltimore

Happy are those who observe justice, who do righteousness at all times.

~ Psalm 106:3 (NRSV)

Check-in

Ask about everyone's week, along with prayer requests for joys and sorrows.

Open with Prayer

Introduction to the *Tearing Down Fences in Baltimore* Video

Bishop Cynthia Moore-KoiKoi shares her experiences in the broader context of racial strife in the video *Tearing Down Fences in Baltimore*. Through the lens of her service and experience as a United Methodist district superintendent in racially torn Baltimore, she challenges viewers to reach out and build relationships in their respective communities. She prophetically calls to all of us in the church to be sources of hope and redemption to communities in conflict. We are all called to be a witness to the love and justice of God in the midst of civil unrest and protest in embattled places like Baltimore.

Video

Watch *Tearing Down Fences in Baltimore*, http://www.gcorr.org/video/building-bridges-to -community-with-the-rev-cynthia-moore-koikoi-2/ (14:12)

Discussion Questions

1. How can prayer walks be uplifting to those praying and those being prayed for in the community? How can we frame our prayers, including prayer walks, for ethnic-specific and multicultural communities?
2. What are the barriers that may be stopping the church from moving forward in urban communities?
3. How has the "fence," both figurative and literal, created barriers that led to and continues with civil unrest and protest against racism in Baltimore?
4. What role does the church play in erecting and supporting fences/barriers? How can we tear down those fences? What are the institutional fences in The United Methodist Church as a denomination?
5. How did fences come down when Christian leadership walked and prayed through Baltimore? How was community created? What was the importance of hope in one of the outcomes of prayer and community?
6. What are you prepared to do in response to racism in this nation and in our churches? How can we fully support urban ministries and the pastors in those ministries and by extension be a strong beacon for equality, identifying the fences?

Closing Prayer in Unison

Light a candle as a reminder of the Holy Spirit's presence.

Creator God, our provider, we humbly seek You as we agree to continue to speak up and be active against the sin of racism. Help us to be strong in what is a difficult journey. Lift up everyone in this group as we continue to learn about and act against racism and work toward reconciliation and justice. Amen.

You shall be called the repairer of the breach, the restorer of streets to live in.

~ Isaiah 58:12b (NRSV)

Resources

Books

Alexander, Michelle. *The New Jim Crow*: Mass Incarceration in the Age of Colorblindness.

Douglas, Kelly Brown. *Stand Your Ground: Black Bodies and the Justice of God*.

Coates, Ta-Nehisi. *Between the World and Me*.

de la Torre, Miguel A. *The Politics of Jesús: A Hispanic Political Theology*.

DeYmaz, Mark and Oneya Fennell Okuwobi. *The Multi-Ethnic Christian Life Primer: An Eight Week Guide to Walking, Working and Worshipping God Together as One*.

DiAngelo, Robin. *What Does It Mean to Be White?: Developing White Racial Literacy*.

Harvey, Jennifer. *Dear White Christians: For Those Still Longing for Racial Reconciliation*.

Irving, Debby. *Waking Up White, and Finding Myself in the Story of Race*.

Johnson, Allan G. *Power, Privilege, and Difference*.

Lee, Enid, et al. *Beyond Heroes and Holidays: A Practical Guide to K-12 Anti-Racist, Multicultural Education and Staff Development*.

Takaki, Ronald. *A Different Mirror: A History of Multicultural America*.

Tatum, Beverly. *Why Are All the Black Kids Sitting Together in the Cafeteria: And Other Conversations about Race*.

Tochluk, Shelly. *Witnessing Whiteness: The Need to Talk About Race and How to Do It*.

Walden, Ken J. and Vergel, L. Lattimore III. *Practical Theology for Church Diversity: A Guide for Clergy and Congregations*.

Watson, Benjamin and Ken Petersen. *Under Our Skin: Getting Real About Race—and Getting Free from the Fears and Frustrations That Divide Us*.

Wise, Tim. *White Like Me: Reflections on Race from a Privileged Son*.

Websites

Robin DiAngelo's website: http://robindiangelo.com

GCORR resources: http://gcorr.org/resources

Shelly Tochluk's website: http://shellytochluk.com

Peggy McIntosh's "*White Privilege: Unpacking the Invisible Knapsack*": https://www.deanza.edu/faculty/lewisjulie/White%20Priviledge%20Unpacking%20the%20Invisible%20Knapsack.pdf

About the Study Guide Author

Dr. Dianne Glave

Dr. Dianne Glave is coordinator of diversity development and inclusion for the Western Pennsylvania Annual Conference of The United Methodist Church.

She completed her master of divinity degree at Candler School of Theology at Emory University and earned a Ph.D. in history. She served as pastor of local congregations before taking her current position. She has also served as a professor in African-American and ethnic studies.

Her publications include *Rooted in the Earth: Reclaiming the African American Environmental Heritage* and *To Love the Wind and the Rain: African American and Environmental History*.

Credits

Amplified Bible (AMP), copyright © 2015 by the Lockman Foundation, La Habra, CA 90631; all rights reserved.
The Message (MSG), copyright © 1993, 1994, 1995, 1996, 2000, 2001, 2002 by Eugene H. Peterson.
New Revised Standard Version (NRSV), copyright © 1989 the Division of Christian Education of the National Council of the Churches of Christ in the United States of America; used by permission; all rights reserved.

Executive Producer: Erin M. Hawkins, General Secretary, General Commission on Religion and Race
Supervising Producer: M. Garlinda Burton
Producer: Henri Giles
Production services provided by United Methodist Communications;
Director of Production: Harry Leake
Study Guide Writers: Dr. Dianne Glave (Series 1) and Dr. G. Faye Wilson (Series 2 and 3)

CPSIA information can be obtained
at www.ICGtesting.com
Printed in the USA
BVOW09s2006140417

481254BV00004B/8/P